Stand STRONG

Part Three: Shayla Learns to Use the Accountability Pathway

Cool stuff for college (and life)!

A College Survival Guidebook With Practices For Your Success

Luckett Davidson

Copyright © 2020 Luckett Davidson

A TouchStone Publication

ALL RIGHTS RESERVED

No part of this book may be translated, used, or reproduced in any form or by any means, in whole or in part, electronic or mechanical, including photocopying, recording, taping, or by any information storage or retrieval system without express written permission from the author or the publisher, except for the use in brief quotations within critical articles and reviews.

www.touchstoneguides.com, luckett@touchstoneguides for additional resources

Limits of Liability and Disclaimer of Warranty:

The authors and/or publisher shall not be liable for misuse of this material.
The contents are strictly for informational and educational purposes only.

Printed and bound in the United States of America
ISBN: 978-1-7333434-2-8

"The moment when a person takes the wheel. That's when adulthood begins."

—David Brooks, New York Times

SHAYLA

Stand STRONG, Part Three

SHAYLA'S Story and the ACCOUNTABILITY PATHWAY

CONTENTS

Pages 2–20 The STORY

About Shayla and her first semester in college

Pages 21–30 EXPLORE Your Own Story

Questions for you to think about and answer that'll help you do well in college and beyond

Pages 8–18, 33 ACCOUNTABILITY PATHWAY

You can use it to hold yourself and others accountable without shame, blame or punishment

Pages 28–29 COMMIT

Set a **Big Goal** that you can commit to and plan some steps you can take to reach that goal

Hi, girls. Time for bed.
Oh, boy...
SHAY! SHAY!
Shay Shay! Play with me.
After the girls are asleep.

Accountability Pathway

Who me? — Yes me!

UNACCOUNTABLE

CLUELESS
- unaware
- asleep
- unconcerned

BLAME OTHERS
- they won't listen
- I did it
- won't let me
- said no

I CAN'T / EXCUSES
- no time
- it's too big
- I'm too small

WAIT AND HOPE
- maybe it will go away
- fix itself

ACCOUNTABLE

GET REAL
- Wake up

IT'S UP TO ME
- Take the wheel
- I got this!

FIND A WAY
- Partner
- Brainstorm
- Break it down

GO FOR IT!

Not shame or blame / punishment
- Learning is Choice
- Awareness
- Growth

Talk to Action from
- Powerful Questions
- Mindful Presence — useful
- Review Progress

- Learn from Each Step
- Apply Past Lessons
- Partners

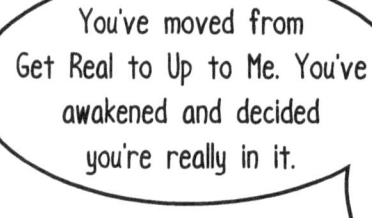

THE FOLLOWING WEEK

"We both got an A!"

If it's meant to be It's Up to Me.

DEZ

"I gotta go now. I've made a date to talk to my folks. I think they can help me deal with my crazy schedule."

Here're some things I learned.

* I'm pretty good at handling a lot of different things, but I still need to stop and think about what I'm doing.

* I have to be honest with myself about what's Up to Me.

* College isn't like high school, and I need new ways of doing things.

* A tool like the Accountability Pathway can help me figure it out.

* It helps to break things down into smaller, timely steps.

* It's fun to celebrate with a friend before I go on to the next step.

What situations did Shayla face in her first semester in college?
What do you think she learned?
Write and draw and share……

EXPLORE YOUR OWN STORY

with

the ACCOUNTABILITY PATHWAY

_____
(YOUR NAME)

Learns to use the Accountability Pathway

_____
(DATE)

Stand STRONG, Part Three

> As you answer the questions, look at your own habits of thought and action. How do they support your goals? What needs to change?

> You'll find some questions about your accountability. You can work with them here and now.

WHAT YOU'LL NEED:

* This book
* Willingness to think about your own story
* Pen or pencil
* Colored pencils or markers

WHAT YOU'LL DO:

* Make notes and images about something in your life. (You may want to use your BIG dream or another goal)
* Center yourself. You learned how in Part One of Stand STRONG (see page 34)
* Use Powerful Questions from Part Two to locate yourself on the Accountability Pathway (see page 35)
* Consider where you are on the Accountability Pathway
* Locate yourself on the Pathway and plan small steps to move toward Go For It.
* Share your thoughts and plans with someone like a classmate or mentor

TAKE THE WHEEL

WHO ME? YES ME!

Name and draw the one thing you'd like to think about today. It can be your DREAM or one of the goals you set for yourself in Part One or something else in your life.

My DREAM is to become a poet. But for now, my Big Goal is getting an A in my literature class.

How would it feel to take some steps toward your dream or your goal? Write and draw...

Now let's look at the Accountability Pathway and where you are in regard to your goal.
Name and draw some ways you are UNACCOUNTABLE
for action toward your goal.

Some things I've experienced myself:

* I got overwhelmed by the work and made excuses.
* I blamed my teacher when I fell asleep in class.
* I was in a rush all the time and didn't stop to think.
* I played with my sisters instead of getting them (and me) to bed on time.

When will you wake up and Get Real? What will happen when you do?
Write and draw.

These are some things that happened for me:

* I realized early in the semester that I was overextended.
* I admitted that I was Blaming Others for something that is my responsibility.
* I became willing to be Accountable.
* I started to think that "It's Up To Me."
* I recognized my high school teacher's Accountability Pathway drawing as something to be curious about and asked her to explain it.

Now that you've awakened to your situation, how can you move through the Pathway and Go For It?
Write and draw 2 or 3 images about how you could change your thinking and do things differently.

Here are some ideas to get you started.

* Realize it's MY responsibility to do well
* Break down my goal into smaller steps
* Recognize what's most important right now
* Brainstorm some solutions
* Ask for help
* Do some research to find solutions

Rewrite your Big Goal here. If it has changed,
be sure to change the language here.

Here's how I've fine-tuned my goal:

Even though my Dream is to be a poet, my Big Goal for now is getting an A in literature class. Making an A on the test was a step that got me closer to my Big Goal.

Look over the questions you've answered.
Then break your Big Goal down into smaller steps.

Which of your small steps will you commit to doing next week?
Write and draw and share.

"Locating myself on the PATHWAY helps me get a handle on how my actions support my goals—or don't."

Here's what I want to do next week. →

By when? →

What or who will help me be Accountable? →

WAY TO GO!

You've just completed Part Three of Stand STRONG,
a series that will help you navigate new experiences
and stay calm in the midst of major changes.

You can use the tools, practices and concepts
to survive college and create the life
you want in college and beyond.

Draw a picture of yourself

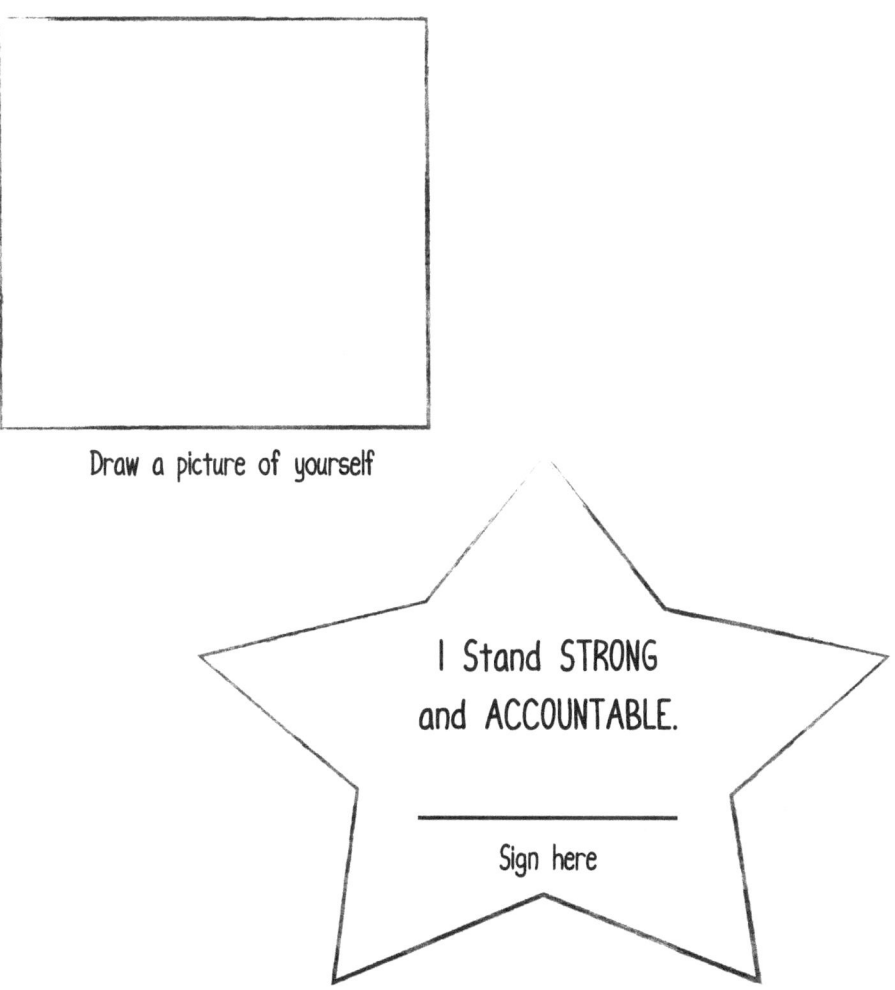

I Stand STRONG
and ACCOUNTABLE.

Sign here

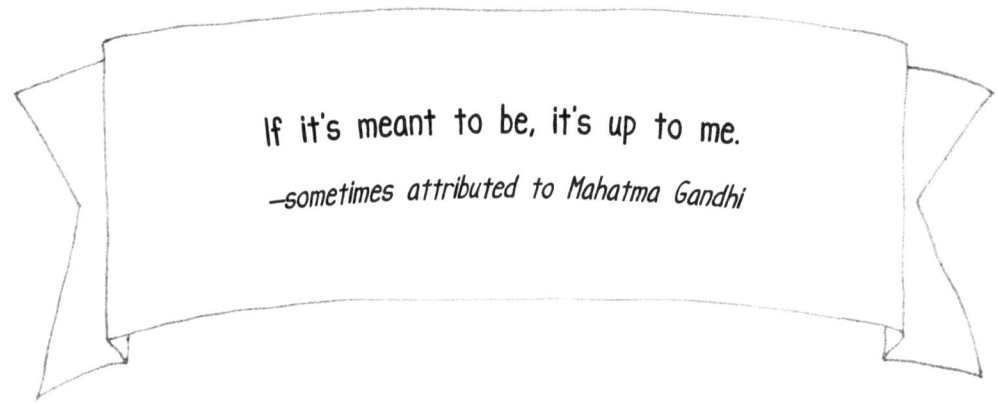

If it's meant to be, it's up to me.

—sometimes attributed to Mahatma Gandhi

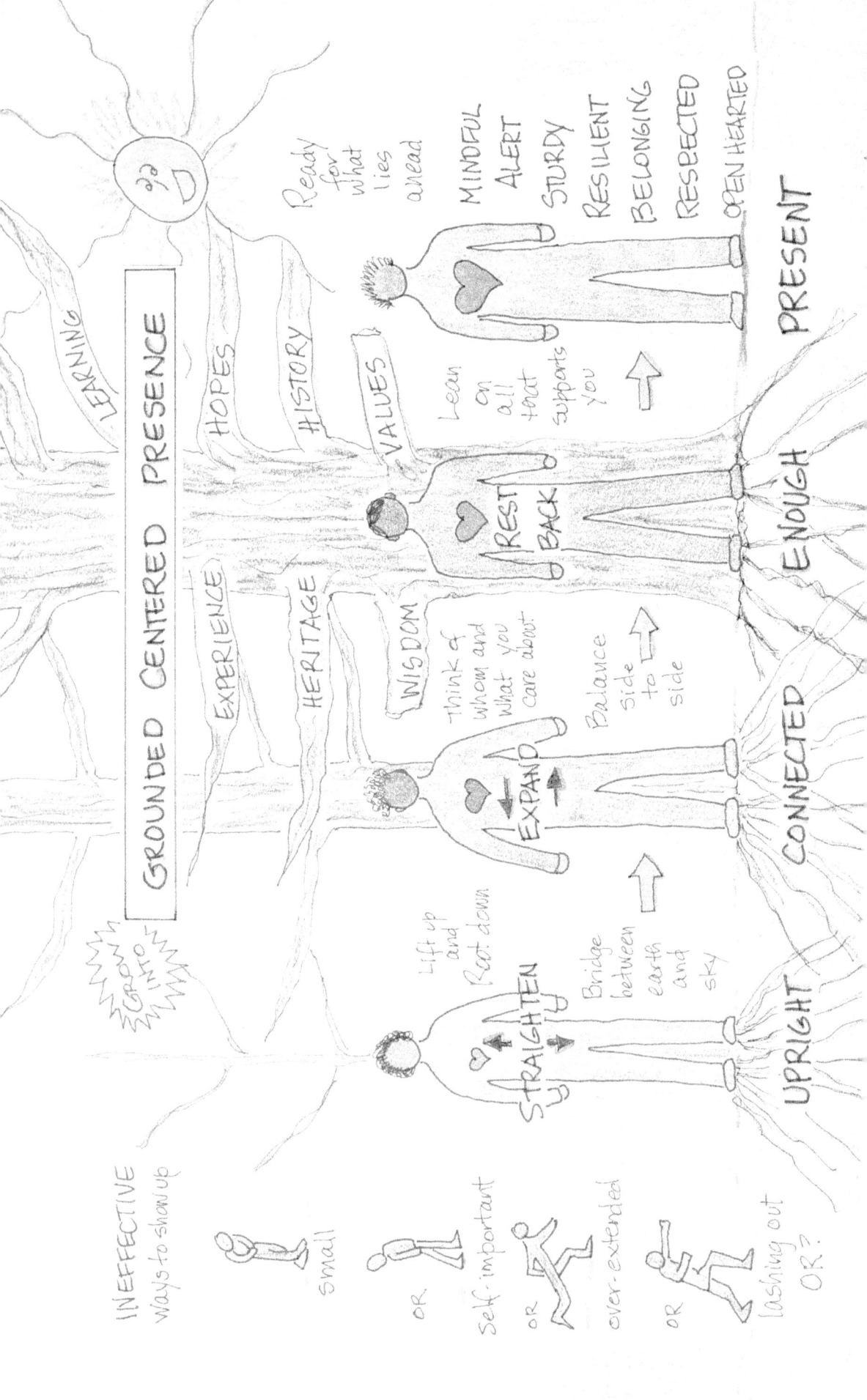

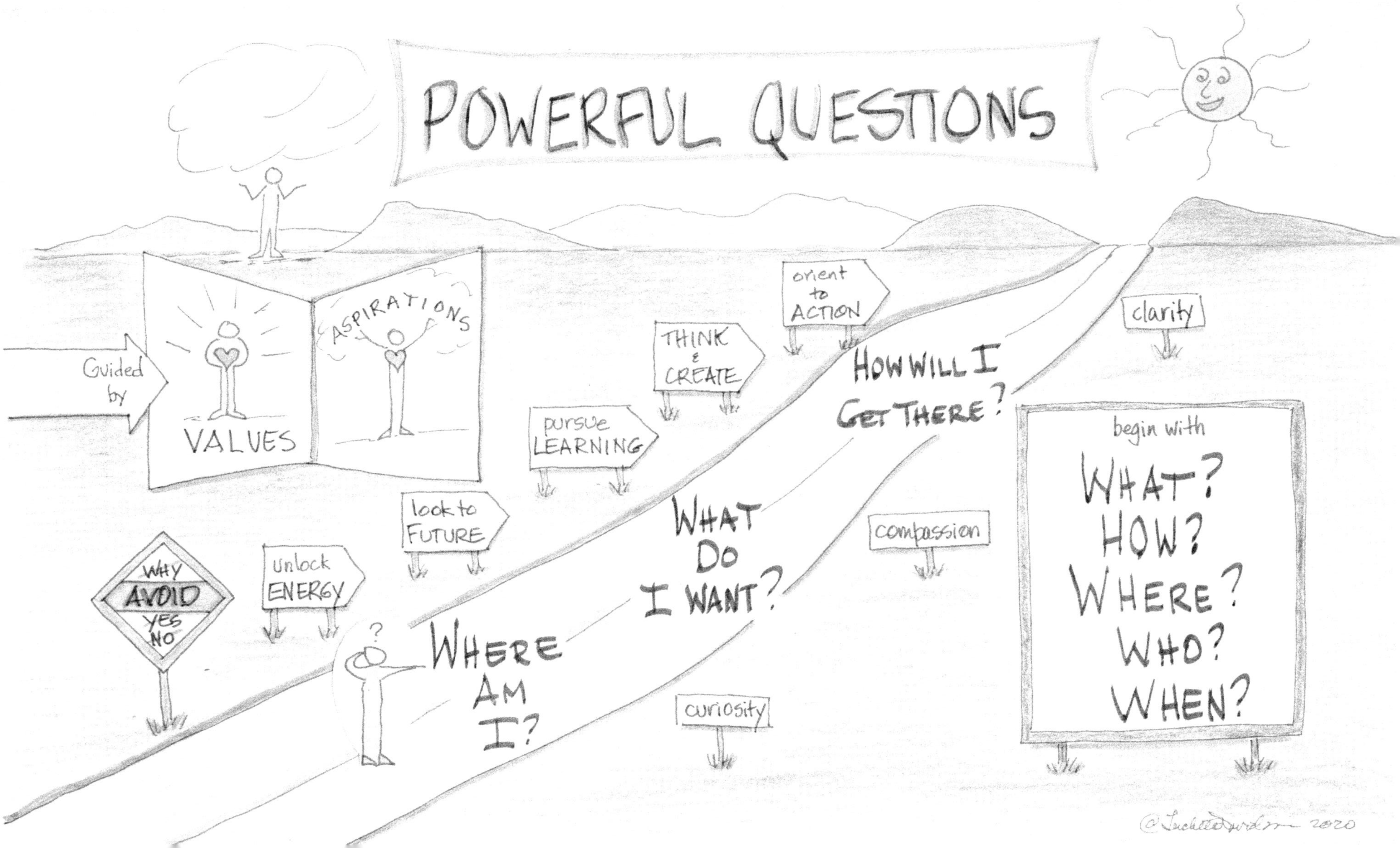

Powerful Questions

begin with
WHAT?
HOW?
WHERE?
WHO?
WHEN?

- clarity
- compassion
- curiosity

How will I get there?

What do I want?

Where am I?

- orient to action
- think & create
- pursue learning
- look to future
- unlock energy
- why avoid yes/no

Aspirations

Values

Guided by

GRATITUDE

Kentucky Foundation for Women
Network Center for Community Change
Doug Silsbee & Bebe Hansen, Presence-Based Coaching®
Jill Adams and Change Makers, Jefferson Community and Technical College
Christy Metzger, First Year Experience, University of Louisville
Alexandra Thrustone, St. Francis School
Janelle Rae, Spalding University
Amy Hirschy, University of Louisville
Lisa Millsaps, Western High School
Tofte Lake Center and Liz Engleman
Jean Johnson and Barbara Hulburt
Lyedie Geer, Practicing Artists Lab
Grace Christiansen and David Temin
Guy Davidson and John Catlett
Elizabeth Neyman and Alex Haynes
Frank Steele, Editor
Karen Abney
Amari and Althea Dryden
Bethany Kelly, Publishing Partner
Stefan Merour, Graphic designer

Danica Novgorodoff, graphic novelist
Keith Look
Mikki and David Little
Amanda Blake, Embright
Shelton McElroy
Cassandra Webb
Mimi Zinniel
Liza Little
Jan Calvert
Ebony O'Rea
Nola and McGee Catlett
Jennie Jean Davidson
Steve Woodring
Witters
Rowing Sisters
Sarah Halley
Carey Goldstein
Jessica Bellamy
Pam Greenwell
Julie Wunderlin
Last Thursday Book Club

CITATION

Poetry Excerpts: Gwendolyn Brooks, "Truth," *Blacks*, 1987.
Accountability Pathway, adapted from the Accountability Continuum
Jolie Bain Pillsbury, Sherbrooke Consulting

Luckett Davidson, a leadership development coach, writer and illustrator, lives with her family in Louisville, Kentucky.

Luckett's take on the personal skills required for college survival is grounded in her studies and explorations in Presence-Based Coaching®, community organizing, the food industry, and fine arts as well as lived experience.

Touchstone Guides presents **Stand STRONG**, a series that supports students through the transition from high school to college. This unique, interactive series allows students to personalize their growth by reflecting and practicing new skills and habits of self-awareness and leadership presence.

In **Part One**, Coleman learns to Center and watches his confidence soar.

In **Part Two**, Will learns to ask Powerful Questions as he considers big and small decisions.

In **Part Three**, Shayla learns how the Accountability Pathway can help her make progress toward major goals.

Join them as they journey through the challenges of college and learn to build inner strength, seek support and stand strong!

Visit our website www.touchstoneguides.com to download the Stand Strong Tips for Session Leaders. These handy tips support those wishing to lead a small group! Posters are also available on the website for purchase.

Bulk and nonprofit rates are available. Contact us for more information at luckett@touchstoneguides.com.

Touchstone Guides explore the intersection of coaching skills, practices and accessible and memorable images. Compassion, resonance, grace and resilience are the touchstones of our work.

www.ingramcontent.com/pod-product-compliance
Lightning Source LLC
Chambersburg PA
CBHW081129080526
44587CB00021B/3809